ME, YOU, US
a book to fill out together

BEST
FRIENDS

LISA CURRIE
A TARCHERPERIGEE BOOK

tarcherperigee

an imprint of Penguin Random House LLC
penguinrandomhouse.com

ISBN: 9780593421611
Proprietary ISBN: 9781101949832

Printed in the United States of America
1st Printing

Dedicated to <u>Shannon Keane</u>

Paint on your shorts.
Basketball tucked under your arm.
Pointing out the swirl of colors in a sunset.
Every day I feel lucky to have been your friend.

♡

welcome!

This is a creative space to share with your best friend.

✿ Daydream about the exciting places life could take you!

✿ Brainstorm ideas for your matching tattoos!

✿ Plan a celebration together!

✿ Doodle your friendship story, page by page!

And the best part? As you fill out the book together, ME, YOU, US will become an amazing time capsule to look back on and treasure.

It's the most special thing having a friend to share life with. Enjoy some "us time" together in these pages!

xo lisa

LET'S BEGIN!

In this book there are no rules and definitely no such thing as a wrong answer. Just flip to a random page and use the prompts to jot down whatever silly thoughts or sweet memories pop into your brain.

Chat about it together. Or just doodle quietly side by side. Non-awkward silences can be the best, no?

At the top of each page there's a space (ME: You: US:) to share how you're each feeling today, the nicknames you give each other, or whatever else pops into your mind!

SUPPLY LIST

Pens are a good place to start. But why not get extra playful? Rustle up some colored pencils and markers. Find that set of glitter pens you once bought. Share your favorite art supplies with each other. Even collect magazines and photos to cut out and scrapbook over the pages. Have some fun with it!

ME: _Rylee_ WHEN: _8:38 pm_
YOU: _Elaina_ WHERE: _Holland_
US: _Besties_

why I chose you
as my best friend

you have pretty ginger hair

your humor

We swim

your kindness

ME: _____ WHEN: _____

YOU: _____ WHERE: _____

US: _____

a dream we both share & are headed toward

ME: _____ WHEN: _____

You: _____ WHERE: _____

US: _____

the story we'll tell when we're old and gray

remember
that time we...

ME: _____   WHEN: _____
YOU: _____   WHERE: _____
US: _____

how we keep our friendship healthy

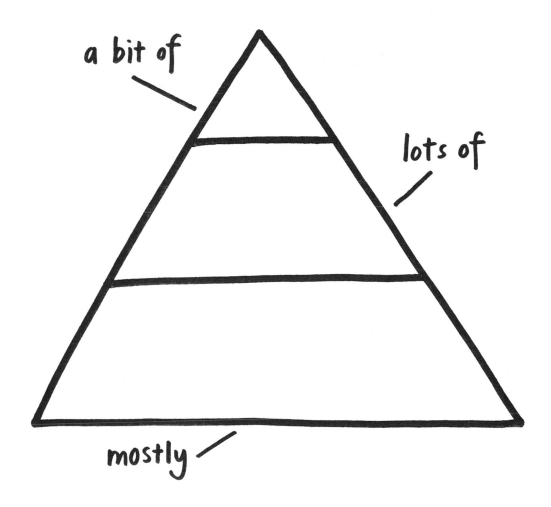

a bit of

lots of

mostly

ME: _____   WHEN: _____

YOU: _____   WHERE: _____

US: _____

challenges we helped each other through

1.

2.

3.

LEVEL COMPLETE!

ME: _____   WHEN: _____
YOU: _____   WHERE: _____
US: _____

things we never get bored of

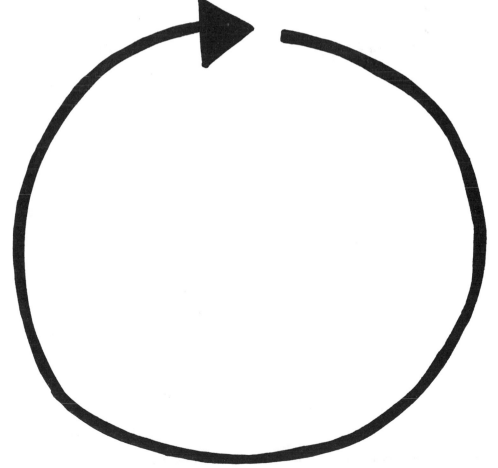

ME: _____   WHEN: _____

YOU: _____   WHERE: _____

US: _____

a cheeky lie we've told

ME: _____ WHEN: _____

YOU: _____ WHERE: _____

US: _____

ideas for our matching tattoos

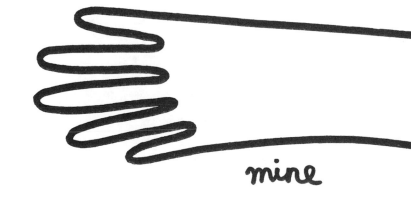

yours

mine

ME: _____   WHEN: _____

You: _____   WHERE: _____

US: _____

last time we had
a two-person party

ME: _____   WHEN: _____

You: _____   WHERE: _____

US: _____

the fictional world
we wish was real

welcome to

ME: _____ WHEN: _____

YOU: _____ WHERE: _____

US: _____

the obsessions we bond over

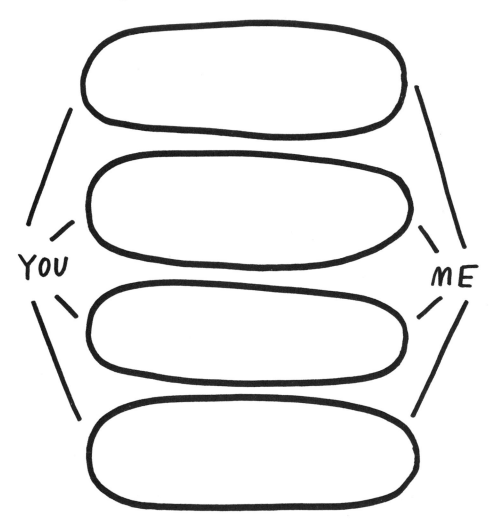

ME: _____ WHEN: _____

You: _____ WHERE: _____

US: _____

our unusual talents

YOURS

MINE

ME: _____ WHEN: _____

You: _____ WHERE: _____

US: _____

a small "thanks" we forgot to tell each other

thank you!

XX

thank you!

XX

ME: _____   WHEN: _____

You: _____   WHERE: _____

US: _____

our wildest dream that we're scared to say aloud

ME: _____ WHEN: _____

You: _____ WHERE: _____

US: _____

if we made our own ice cream flavor

a silly little thing
that is precious to me

$ PRICELESS

$ PRICELESS

ME: _____ WHEN: _____

You: _____ WHERE: _____

US: _____

the thoughts we have
but don't say out loud

ME: _____   WHEN: _____

You: _____   WHERE: _____

US: _____

if we made our own
Public holiday

DAY!

how to celebrate

1.

2.

3.

ME: _____ WHEN: _____

You: _____ WHERE: _____

US: _____

two truths and
one lie about us*

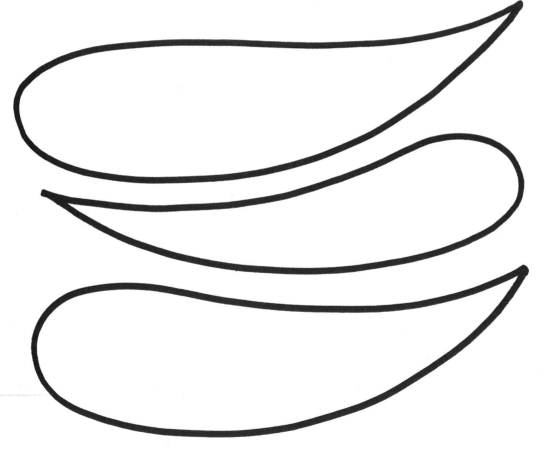

*in no particular order

ME: _____ WHEN: _____

YOU: _____ WHERE: _____

US: _____

the last time we got REALLY EXCITED!!

emergency pep talk from me to you

APPLICABLE FOR:

☐ FIRST DATES   ☐ JOB INTERVIEWS
☐ TOUGH DECISIONS   ☐ _____

ME: _____   WHEN: _____

You: _____   WHERE: _____

US: _____

APPLICABLE FOR:

☐ FIRST DATES   ☐ JOB INTERVIEWS

☐ TOUGH DECISIONS   ☐ _____

ME: _____   WHEN: _____

You: _____   WHERE: _____

US: _____

our #1 move on the dance floor

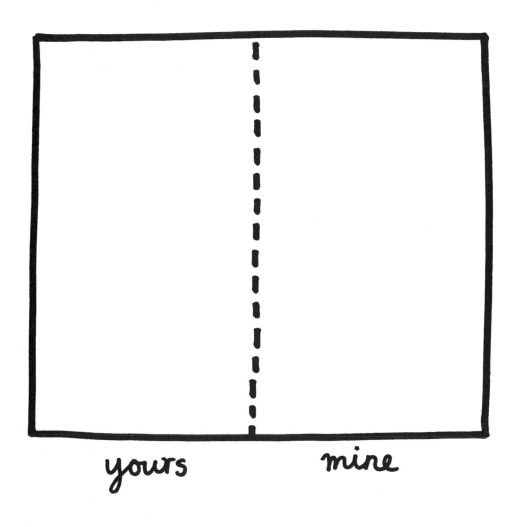

yours   mine

ME: _____ WHEN: _____

You: _____ WHERE: _____

US: _____

next time you visit, please bring...

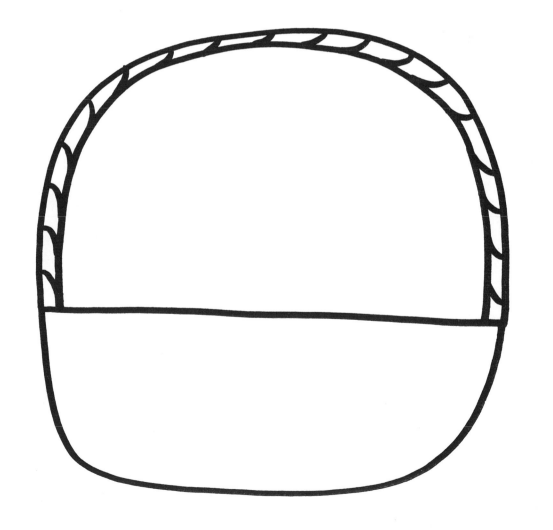

ME: _____   WHEN: _____

You: _____   WHERE: _____

US: _____

ways we refuse to grow up

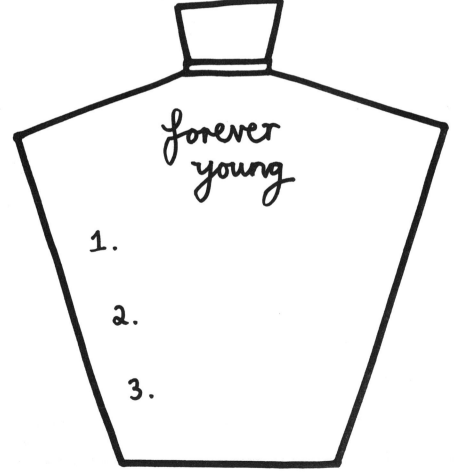

forever young

1.

2.

3.

ME: _____ WHEN: _____

You: _____ WHERE: _____

US: _____

one way our friendship has evolved

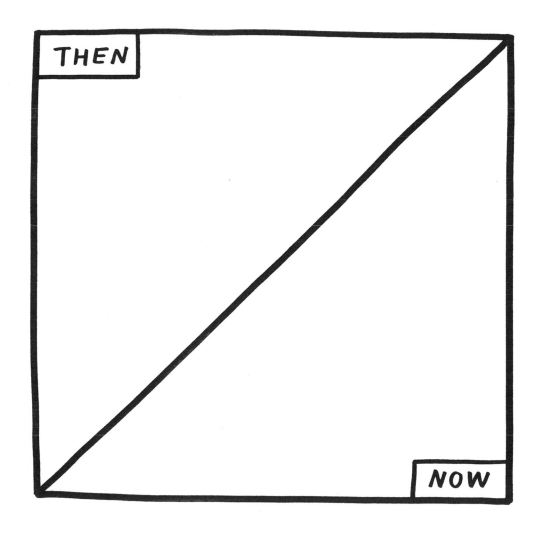

THEN

NOW

ME: _____   WHEN: _____

You: _____   WHERE: _____

US: _____

our secret ingredient

that makes everything better

ME: _____ WHEN: _____

You: _____ WHERE: _____

US: _____

an embarrasing memory
we can laugh about now

yours:

mine:

ME: _____ WHEN: _____

YOU: _____ WHERE: _____

US: _____

new things we've tried recently

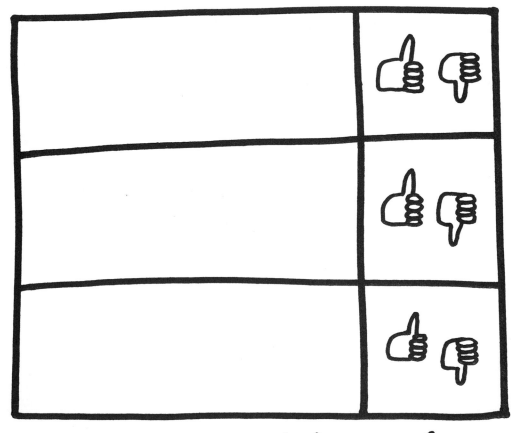

circle one ⤴

ME: _____   WHEN: _____
You: _____   WHERE: _____
US: _____

our perfect movie night

+

snack selection:

ME: _____   WHEN: _____

You: _____   WHERE: _____

US: _____

things we think are HILARIOUS*

* even if no one else does.

ME: _____ WHEN: _____

YOU: _____ WHERE: _____

US: _____

the view from our favorite spot

ME: _____ WHEN: _____

You: _____ WHERE: _____

US: _____

how our music taste has evolved

then :

now :

ME: _____   WHEN: _____

You: _____   WHERE: _____

US: _____

our promises to each other

-
-
-

SIGNED:

&

.... & ....

okay, we'll just agree to disagree

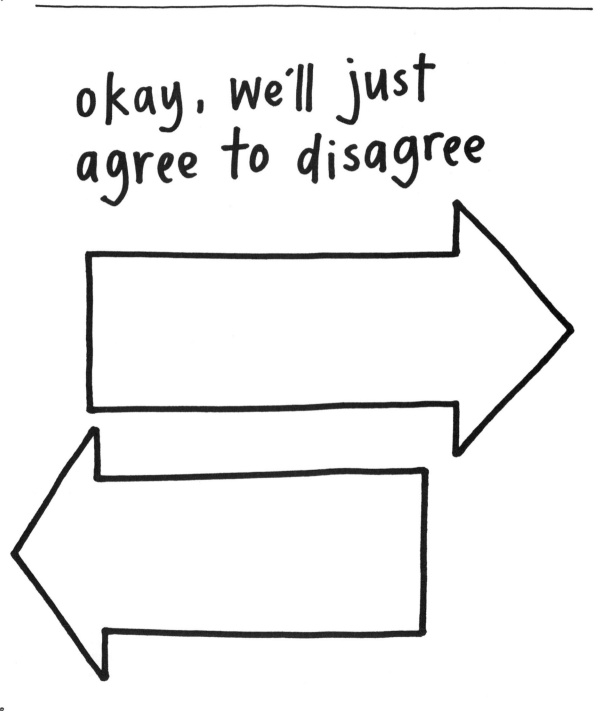

ME: _____ WHEN: _____

You: _____ WHERE: _____

US: _____

a time when I felt
extra close to you

the award I think you deserve

ME: _____ WHEN: _____

You: _____ WHERE: _____

US: _____

your acceptance speech

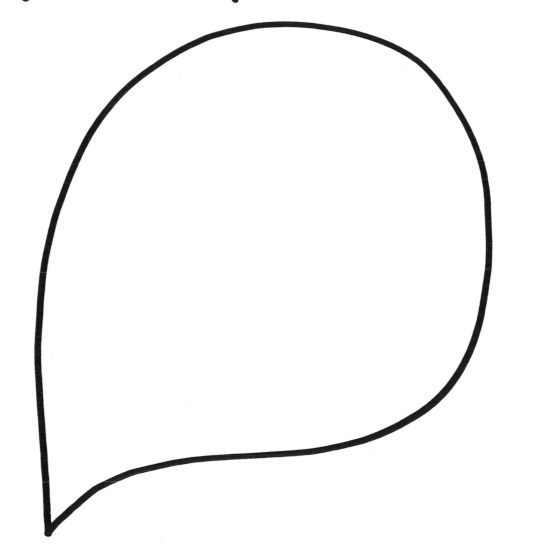

the award you
think I deserve

ME: _____ WHEN: _____

You: _____ WHERE: _____

US: _____

my acceptance speech

ME: _____ WHEN: _____

You: _____ WHERE: _____

US: _____

our motto for life

ME: _____ WHEN: _____

YOU: _____ WHERE: _____

US: _____

how to celebrate our
next friendiversary

ME: _____ WHEN: _____

YOU: _____ WHERE: _____

US: _____

the dinner party
of our dreams

guest list

- you
- me
-
-
-
-
-
-

ME: _____ WHEN: _____

You: _____ WHERE: _____

US: _____

details of a favorite
day together

taste

smell

touch

sound

our status updates

JUST NOW

ONE HOUR AGO

TWO HOURS AGO

YESTERDAY

ME: _____   WHEN: _____
You: _____   WHERE: _____
US: _____

LAST WEEK

TWO MONTHS AGO

SIX MONTHS AGO

ONE YEAR AGO

ME: _____   WHEN: _____

YOU: _____   WHERE: _____

US: _____

the morning reminder
we need to hear

ME: _____ WHEN: _____

YOU: _____ WHERE: _____

US: _____

the name of our secret club

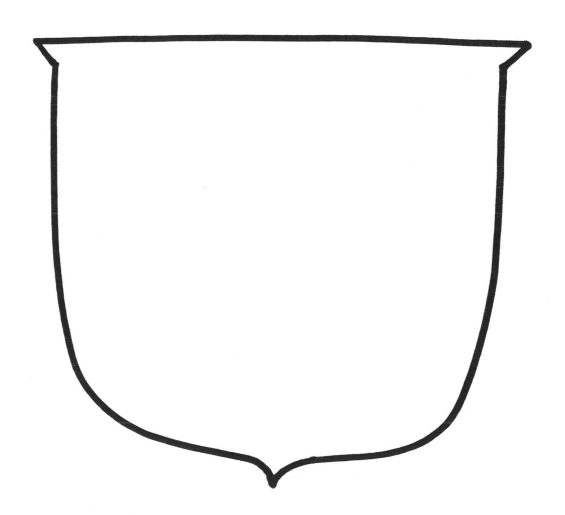

ME: _____   WHEN: _____

You: _____   WHERE: _____

US: _____

the toughest journey we've been on together

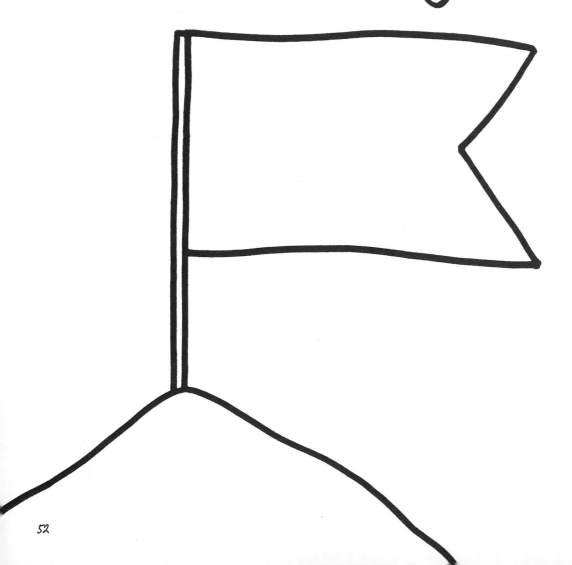

ME: _____ WHEN: _____

YOU: _____ WHERE: _____

US: _____

places we've had the most fun

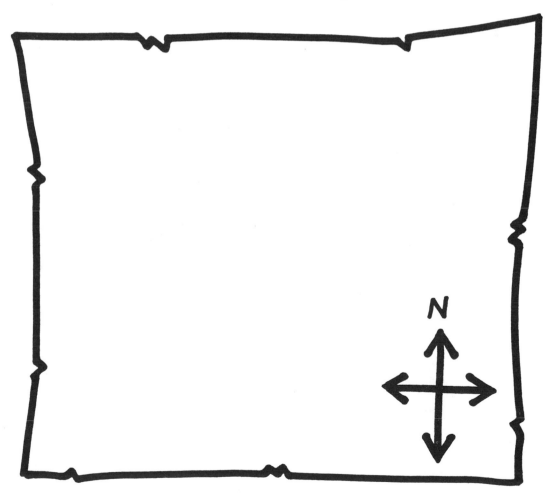

N

the speech I'd give if you were moving overseas

ME: _____ WHEN: _____

YOU: _____ WHERE: _____

US: _____

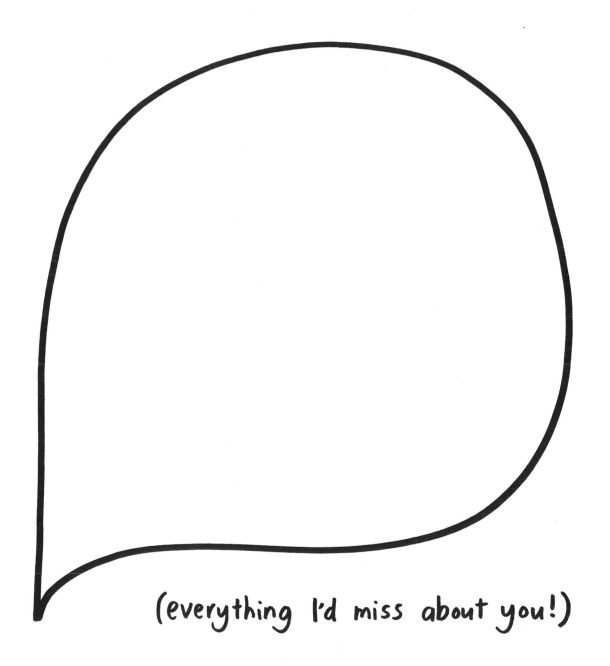

(everything I'd miss about you!)

ME: _____   WHEN: _____

You: _____   WHERE: _____

US: _____

ways we've become the same

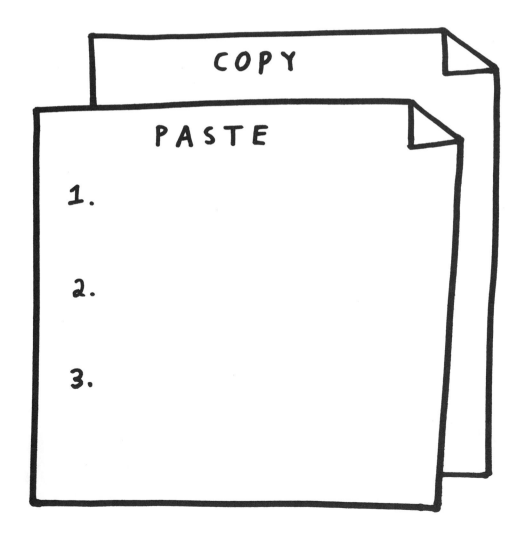

COPY

PASTE

1.

2.

3.

ME: _____ WHEN: _____

YOU: _____ WHERE: _____

US: _____

the closest thing we have to matching outfits

ME: _____ WHEN: _____

You: _____ WHERE: _____

US: _____

little ways we make
each other smile

ME: _____   WHEN: _____

You: _____   WHERE: _____

US: _____

our favorite way to procrastinate

TO DO

SLEEP

ME: _____   WHEN: _____

YOU: _____   WHERE: _____

US: _____

our recent words of wisdom

ME: _____   WHEN: _____

You: _____   WHERE: _____

US: _____

if we were stranded on a deserted island...

OUR ESSENTIALS

highlights of our time together ... so far!

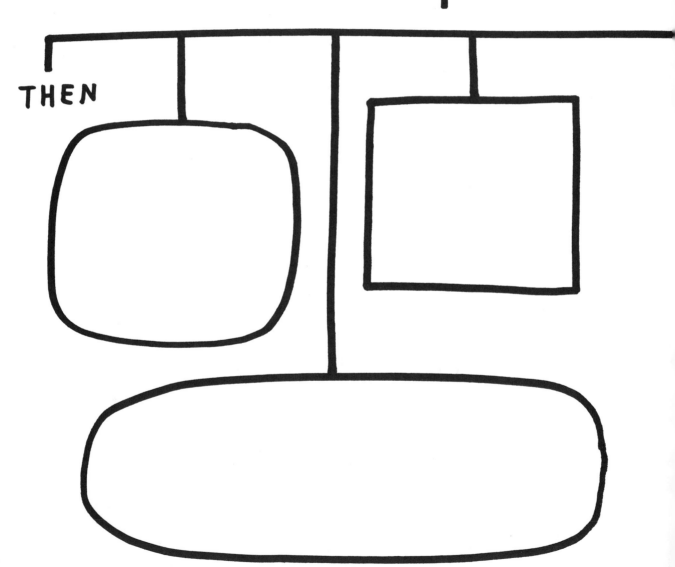

THEN

ME: _____ WHEN: _____

You: _____ WHERE: _____

US: _____

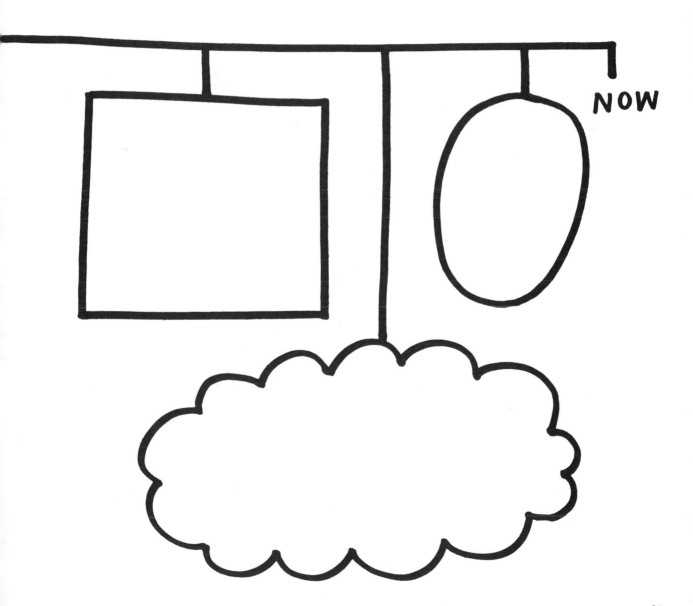

NOW

ME: _____   WHEN: _____

You: _____   WHERE: _____

US: _____

what we protest about

NO MORE

WE WANT

ME: _____   WHEN: _____

YOU: _____   WHERE: _____

US: _____

problems you helped me to untangle

_____

_____

_____

ME: _____   WHEN: _____

You: _____   WHERE: _____

US: _____

your best party trick

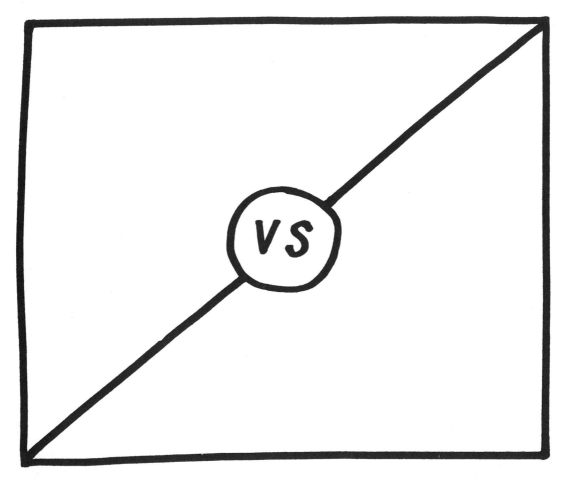

my best party trick

ME: _____ WHEN: _____

You: _____ WHERE: _____

US: _____

things we couldn't wait to tell each other

GOOD NEWS

1.

2.

3.

ME: _____ WHEN: _____

You: _____ WHERE: _____

US: _____

reasons we'd stay up all night together

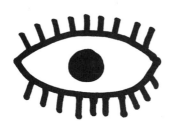 

1.

2.

3.

ME: _____ WHEN: _____

You: _____ WHERE: _____

US: _____

an unexpected perk
of being your friend

FREE!

LIFE TIME
SUPPLY!

ME: _____   WHEN: _____

You: _____   WHERE: _____

US: _____

if a genie gave us three wishes

FIRST
WISH

SECOND
WISH

THIRD
WISH

ME: _____ WHEN: _____

You: _____ WHERE: _____

US: _____

something we're both
still figuring out

HOW TO

ME: _____ WHEN: _____

You: _____ WHERE: _____

US: _____

things that make
us cry

(happy tears & sad tears)

ME: _____   WHEN: _____

YOU: _____   WHERE: _____

US: _____

our favorite ways
to be comforted

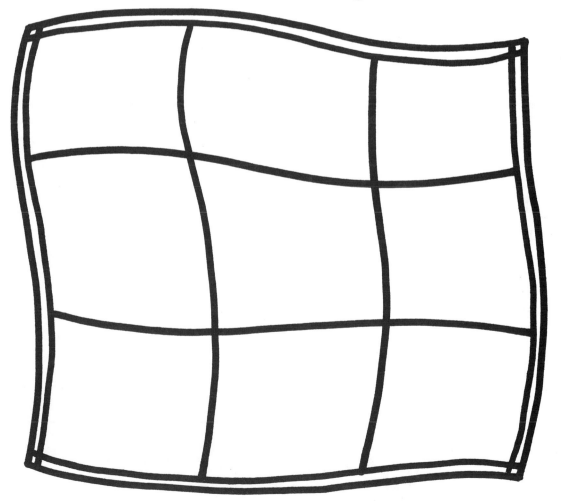

the little ways we
impress each other

YOUR REPORT CARD

A+

A+

A+

ME: _____ WHEN: _____

YOU: _____ WHERE: _____

US: _____

MY REPORT CARD

A+

A+

A+

ME: _____ WHEN: _____

You: _____ WHERE: _____

US: _____

things we were once obsessed with

LOST PROPERTY

ME: _____ WHEN: _____

You: _____ WHERE: _____

US: _____

our most
Frequently Asked Questions

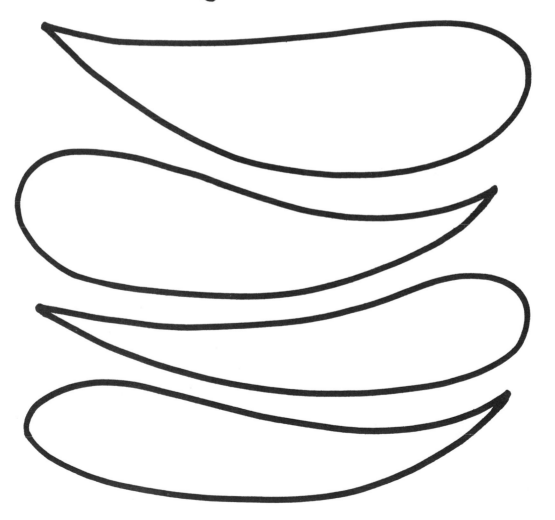

ME: _____ WHEN: _____

You: _____ WHERE: _____

US: _____

the farthest we've ever been from home

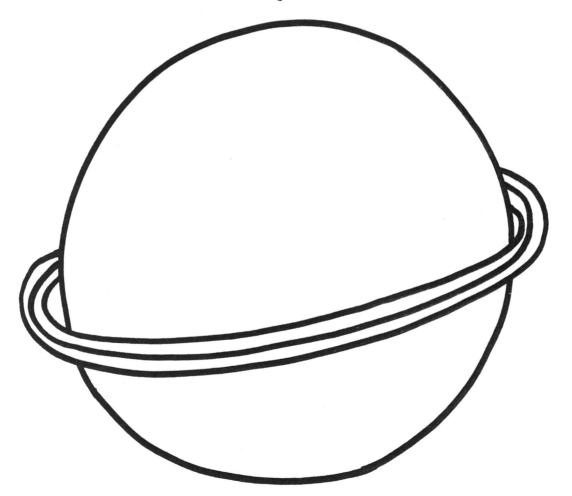

ME: _____ WHEN: _____

YOU: _____ WHERE: _____

US: _____

our favorite game to play

THE RULES

- •
- •
- •

ME: _____ WHEN: _____

YOU: _____ WHERE: _____

US: _____

the cheapest fun we've had together

TOTAL $

ME: _____   WHEN: _____

YOU: _____   WHERE: _____

US: _____

OUR YEARBOOK

YOU

most likely to:

· ·

· ·

most likely to:

ME

· ·

· ·

our mixtapes for each other

listen to this when:

ME: _____   WHEN: _____

YOU: _____   WHERE: _____

US: _____

listen to this when:

ME: _____ WHEN: _____

You: _____ WHERE: _____

US: _____

my idea of fun

your idea of fun

ME: _____ WHEN: _____

YOU: _____ WHERE: _____

US: _____

the team we both play on

ME: _____   WHEN: _____

YOU: _____   WHERE: _____

US: _____

the moment I knew
we'd be friends forever

ME: _____   WHEN: _____
YOU: _____   WHERE: _____
US: _____

what we'll be doing
in 20 years

☐ safe prediction ☐ wild guess

ME: _____   WHEN: _____

YOU: _____   WHERE: _____

US: _____

that thing we said we'd do one day

ME: _____   WHEN: _____

YOU: _____   WHERE: _____

US: _____

small ways we show
each other we care

ME: _____ WHEN: _____

You: _____ WHERE: _____

US: _____

the lyrics we have stuck in our head

ME: _____   WHEN: _____

You: _____   WHERE: _____

US: _____

what we'd (usually) rather be doing

EXIT   EXIT

you   me

ME: _____ WHEN: _____

YOU: _____ WHERE: _____

US: _____

our most casual time together

our most fancy time together

ME: _____ WHEN: _____

You: _____ WHERE: _____

US: _____

the story of how we met

Once upon a time...

ME: _____ WHEN: _____

You: _____ WHERE: _____

US: _____

how we celebrate the weekend

ME: _____ WHEN: _____

YOU: _____ WHERE: _____

US: _____

the last time we had fun trying

PARTICIPATION AWARD

ME: _____ WHEN: _____

You: _____ WHERE: _____

US: _____

our first celebrity crush

☐ 4EVER!
☐ not anymore

☐ 4EVER!
☐ not anymore

ME: _____ WHEN: _____

You: _____ WHERE: _____

US: _____

how I'd describe you
to a stranger

ME: _____   WHEN: _____

YOU: _____   WHERE: _____

US: _____

something we're REALLY looking forward to

COUNTDOWN

| YEARS | MONTHS | DAYS |

ME: _____ WHEN: _____

YOU: _____ WHERE: _____

US: _____

the homework we give each other

watch this:

read this:

search this:

ME: _____   WHEN: _____

You: _____   WHERE: _____

US: _____

a bravery award
for that thing you did!

ME: _____ WHEN: _____

You: _____ WHERE: _____

US: _____

an unspoken rule we both seem to agree on

We Shall

ME: _____   WHEN: _____

You: _____   WHERE: _____

US: _____

how we get ready to go out

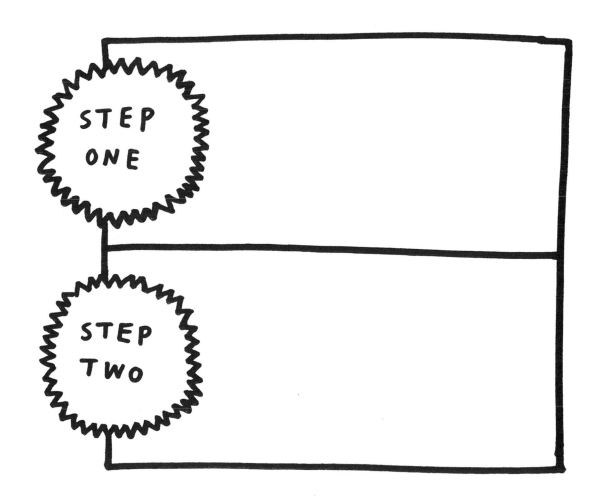

STEP ONE

STEP TWO

ME: _____   WHEN: _____

YOU: _____   WHERE: _____

US: _____

the things we love to chat about lately

ME: _____   WHEN: _____

YOU: _____   WHERE: _____

US: _____

how we cope when we're not together

1.

2.

3.

wish
you
were
Here

xx

our handmade cards
for each other

☐ special occasion   ☐ just because

ME: _____ WHEN: _____

You: _____ WHERE: _____

US: _____

☐ special occasion ☐ just because

ME: _____   WHEN: _____

You: _____   WHERE: _____

US: _____

our own special recipe

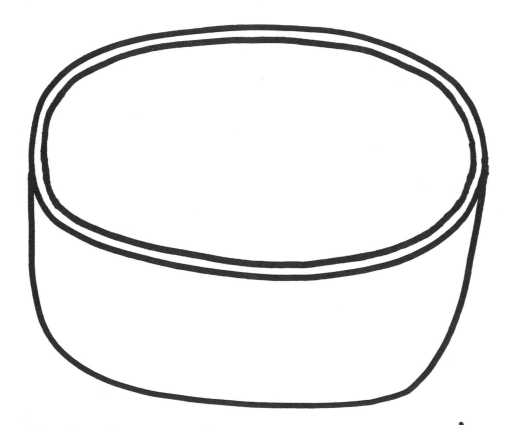

☐ looks good   ☐ tastes good
☐ it's edible   ☐ no comment

ME: _____   WHEN: _____

You: _____   WHERE: _____

US: _____

brands that best describe "us"

UNOFFICIAL
SPONSORS

ME: _____ WHEN: _____

You: _____ WHERE: _____

US: _____

things we miss
about being younger

ME: _____   WHEN: _____

YOU: _____   WHERE: _____

US: _____

what we're wishing for as we get older

ME: _____ WHEN: _____

You: _____ WHERE: _____

US: _____

our recent teamwork

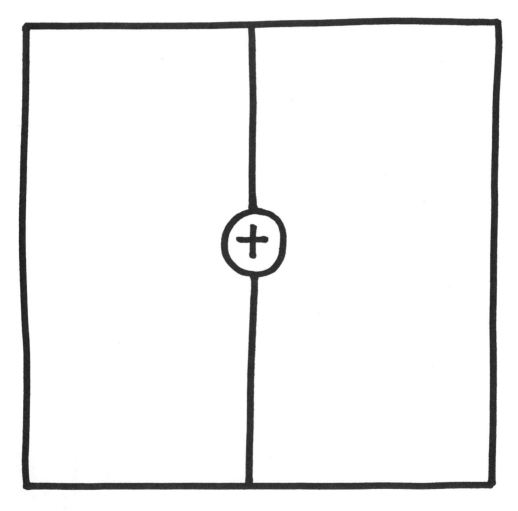

= WE DID IT!!

the internet stuff we send each other

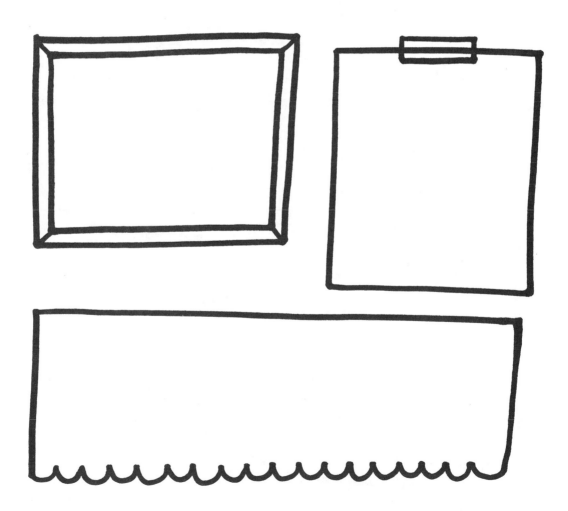

ME: _____ WHEN: _____

YOU: _____ WHERE: _____

US: _____

the catchphrase we're famous for saying

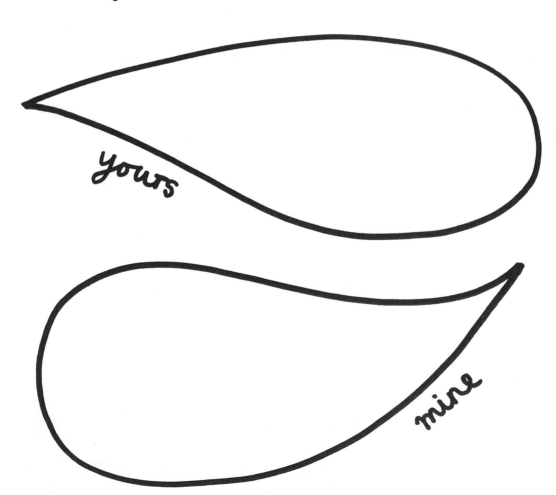

yours

mine

ME: _____ WHEN: _____

YOU: _____ WHERE: _____

US: _____

little milestones we've celebrated together

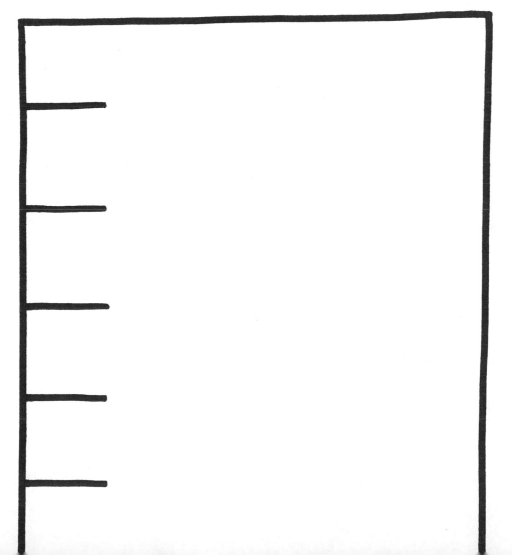

random things that remind me of you

I SPY...

ME: _____ WHEN: _____

YOU: _____ WHERE: _____

US: _____

I SPY...

ME: _____   WHEN: _____

YOU: _____   WHERE: _____

US: _____

the chapters we've had together — so far!

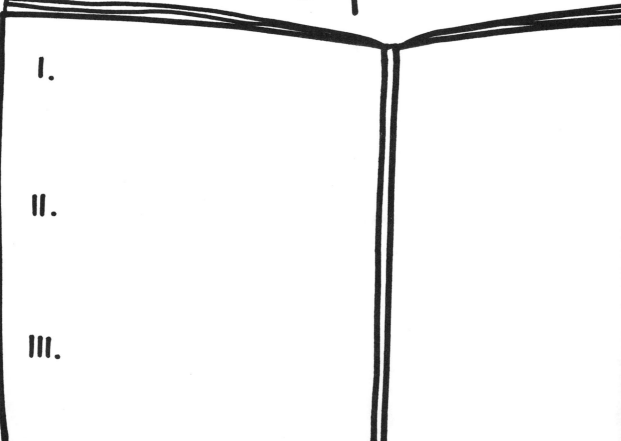

I.

II.

III.

ME: _____   WHEN: _____

You: _____   WHERE: _____

US: _____

the magic potions
We want to take a sip of

ME: _____ WHEN: _____

You: _____ WHERE: _____

US: _____

the challenge we bravely accepted

I DARE YOU...

☐ PASS   ☐ FAIL   ☐ NICE TRY

ME: _____ WHEN: _____

You: _____ WHERE: _____

US: _____

our recent questions about life and love

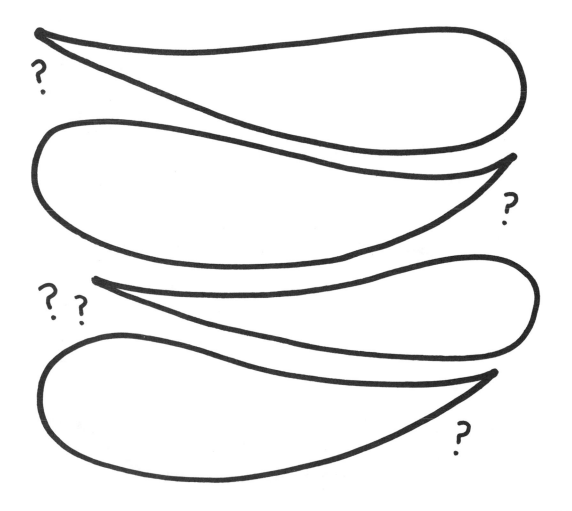

a present we were excited to unwrap

RECENTLY:

AS A CHILD:

ME: _____   WHEN: _____

You: _____   WHERE: _____

US: _____

RECENTLY:

AS A CHILD:

ME: _____ WHEN: _____

You: _____ WHERE: _____

US: _____

my fortune for you

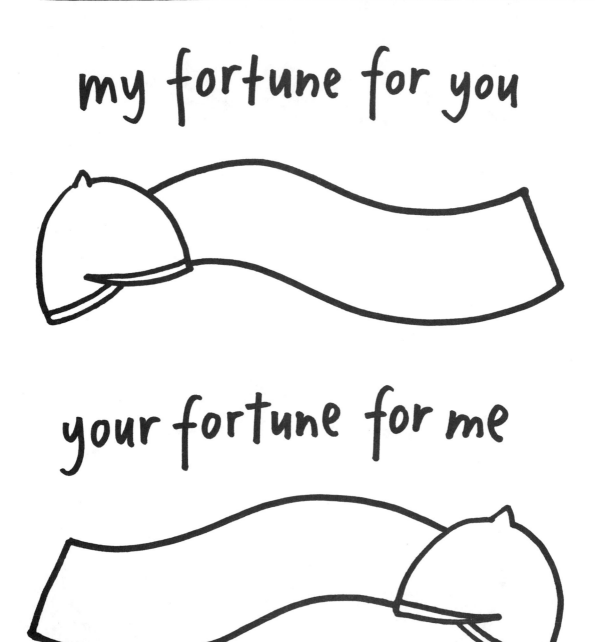

your fortune for me

ME: _____   WHEN: _____

You: _____   WHERE: _____

US: _____

Something we can't wait to celebrate together

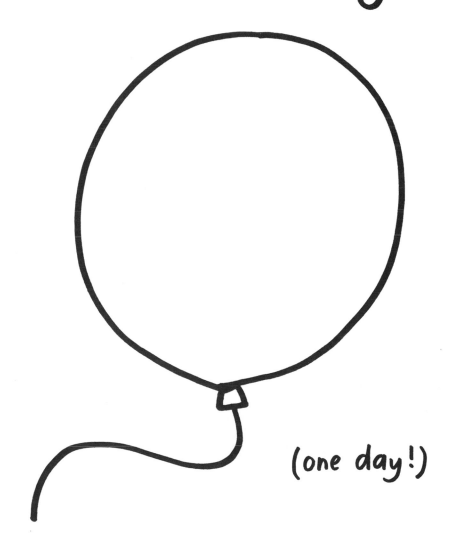

(one day!)

ME: _____ WHEN: _____

YOU: _____ WHERE: _____

US: _____

the book we could write together

☐ SELF-HELP ☐ DIY ☐ COOKBOOK
☐ OTHER _____

ME: _____   WHEN: _____

YOU: _____   WHERE: _____

US: _____

the last time we got FREE STUFF

ME: _____   WHEN: _____

YoU: _____   WHERE: _____

US: _____

things we recently learned about each other

ME: _____   WHEN: _____

You: _____   WHERE: _____

US: _____

our unexplored talents

MIGHT BE GREAT AT

POTENTIAL FOR

FUTURE

ONE DAY!

MAYBE!

ME: _____ WHEN: _____

You: _____ WHERE: _____

Us: _____

the last time we got a bit competitive

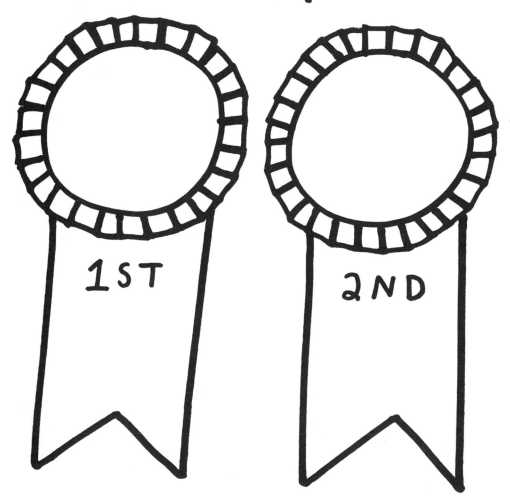

1ST 2ND

ME: _____

You: _____

US: _____

pie chart of how we spend our time together

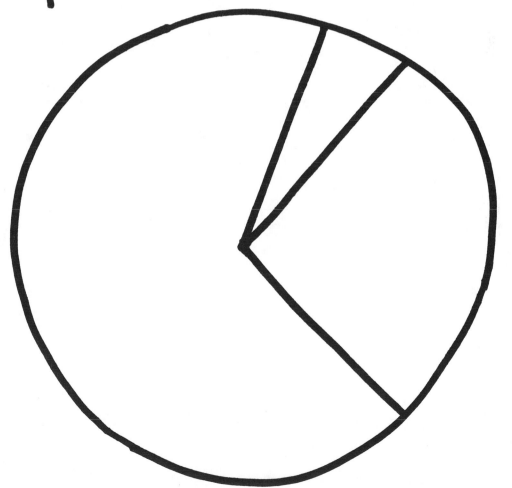

ME: _____ WHEN: _____

YOU: _____ WHERE: _____

US: _____

if Hollywood made a movie about us

TITLE:

STARRING:

as you

as me

ME: _____   WHEN: _____

YOU: _____   WHERE: _____

US: _____

things I most value
your opinion on

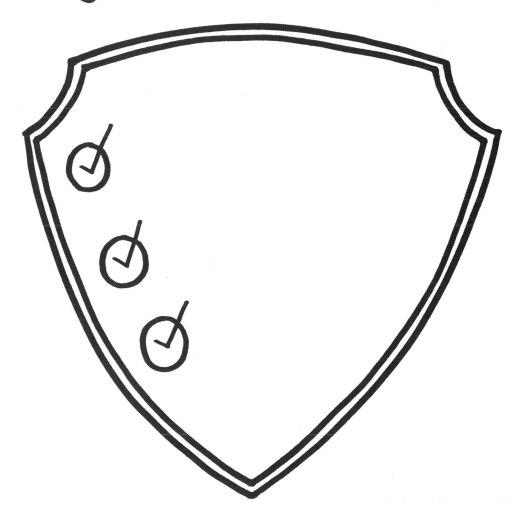

ME: _____ WHEN: _____

YOU: _____ WHERE: _____

US: _____

our ongoing debate

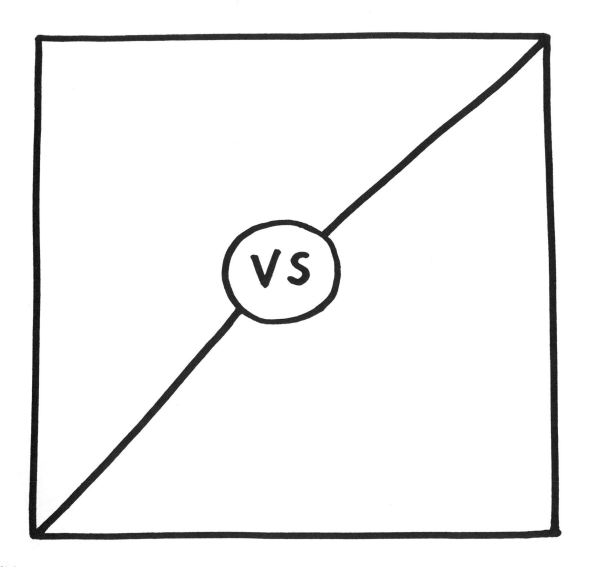

ME: _____   WHEN: _____

You: _____   WHERE: _____

US: _____

our current obsession

ME: _____ WHEN: _____

YOU: _____ WHERE: _____

US: _____

new nicknames for each other

yours   mine

ME: _____ WHEN: _____

You: _____ WHERE: _____

US: _____

if we opened a shop together it'd sell...

ME: _____ WHEN: _____

YOU: _____ WHERE: _____

US: _____

things that happen in our fantasyland

ME: _____ WHEN: _____

YOU: _____ WHERE: _____

US: _____

nobody does this better than us

ME: _____ WHEN: _____

You: _____ WHERE: _____

US: _____

the BIGGEST event
we've been to

and the
smallest
event

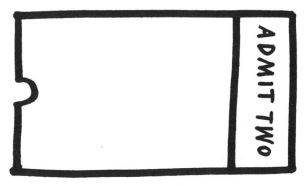

ME: _____   WHEN: _____

You: _____   WHERE: _____

US: _____

tiny details we notice about each other

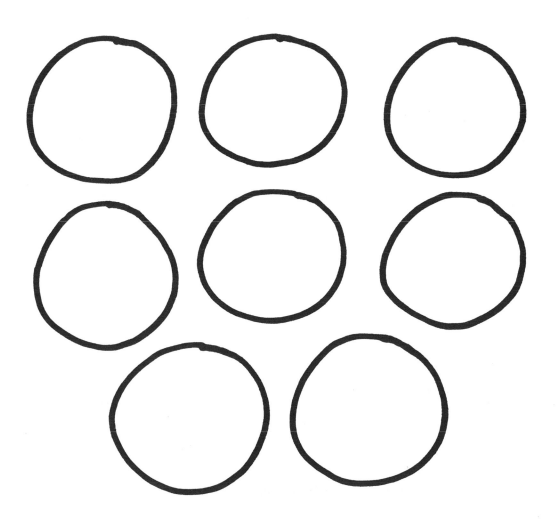

ME: _____   WHEN: _____

YOU: _____   WHERE: _____

US: _____

three things we can both agree on

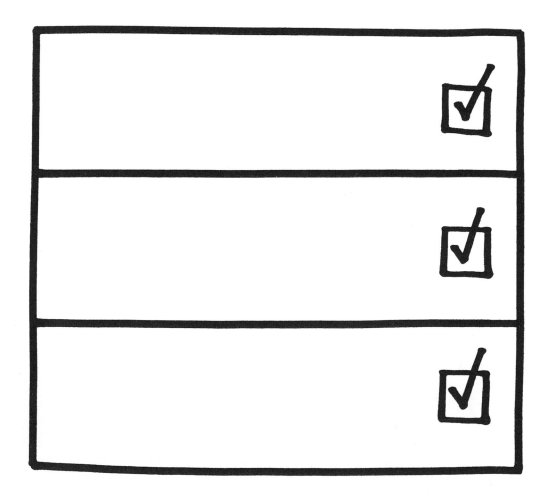

ME: _____ WHEN: _____

You: _____ WHERE: _____

US: _____

the "future selves" we dream about becoming

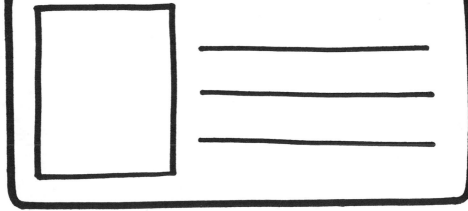

ME: _____   WHEN: _____
You: _____   WHERE: _____
US: _____

the most fun we could have in an hour

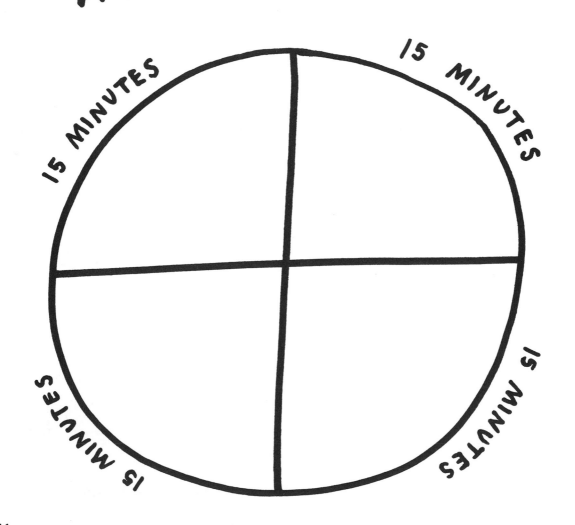

15 MINUTES

15 MINUTES

15 MINUTES

15 MINUTES

ME: _____   WHEN: _____

You: _____   WHERE: _____

US: _____

the last reason we gave each other...

A BIG HUG	
THE GIGGLES	
SOME TOUGH LOVE	
A PEP TALK	

ME: _____   WHEN: _____

You: _____   WHERE: _____

US: _____

nice things we can do for each other

```
┌────────────────────────────────────┐
│  COUPON FOR...                     │
│                                     │
│  _____  │
│                                     │
│  _____  │
│                                     │
│  TO:            FROM:              │
└────────────────────────────────────┘
```

```
┌────────────────────────────────────┐
│  COUPON FOR...                     │
│                                     │
│  _____  │
│                                     │
│  _____  │
│                                     │
│  TO:            FROM:              │
└────────────────────────────────────┘
```

ME: _____ WHEN: _____

YOU: _____ WHERE: _____

US: _____

the scent of our friendship

WITH HINTS OF

_____ & _____

ME: _____   WHEN: _____

YOU: _____   WHERE: _____

US: _____

little things we feel
grateful for today

ME: _____ WHEN: _____

You: _____ WHERE: _____

US: _____

the last time we were partners in crime

WANTED

FOR:

ME: _____ WHEN: _____

You: _____ WHERE: _____

US: _____

instructions for being as cool as we are

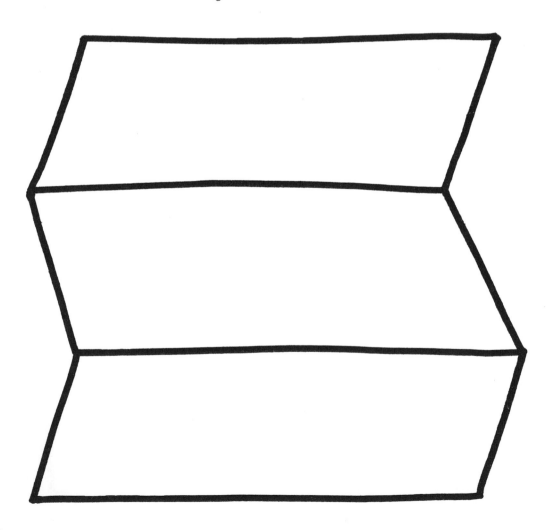

ME: _____ WHEN: _____

You: _____ WHERE: _____

US: _____

a dream we had that came true

ME: _____ WHEN: _____

You: _____ WHERE: _____

us: _____

if we spend too much time together

SIDE EFFECTS

1.

2.

3.

ME: _____ WHEN: _____

You: _____ WHERE: _____

US: _____

a new rule we
Want to introduce

☐ at school   ☐ at work
☐ at parties   ☐ at home

things we like about each other

-
-
-
-

☐ in no particular order
☐ in a very particular order

ME: _____ WHEN: _____

You: _____ WHERE: _____

US: _____

- •
- •
- •
- •

☐ in no particular order
☐ in a very particular order

ME: _____ WHEN: _____

YOU: _____ WHERE: _____

US: _____

how we'd like to
change the world

ME: _____ WHEN: _____

You: _____ WHERE: _____

US: _____

exciting places our life could take us

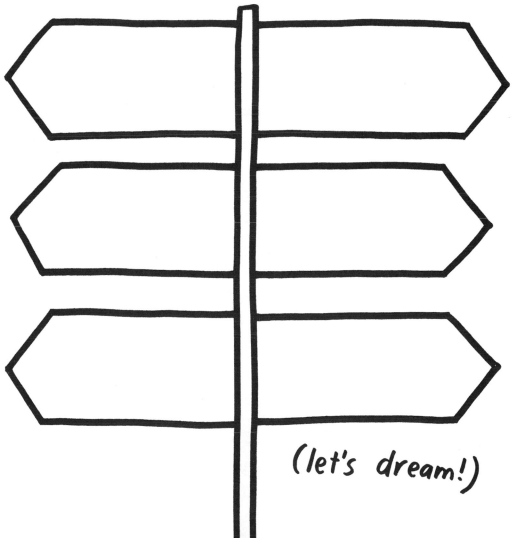

(let's dream!)

ME: _____   WHEN: _____

YOU: _____   WHERE: _____

US: _____

our worst habits
when we're together

1.

2.

3.

4.

*** sorry, everyone!**

ME: _____   WHEN: _____

YOU: _____   WHERE: _____

US: _____

the big event we're getting ready for

ME: _____   WHEN: _____

You: _____   WHERE: _____

US: _____

us as a superhero duo

OUR POWERS

OUR MISSION

ME: _____   WHEN: _____

You: _____   WHERE: _____

US: _____

things we borrow from each other

* with or without permission

ME: _____   WHEN: _____

YOU: _____   WHERE: _____

US: _____

the secret business we do together

Please
DO NOT DISTURB

ME: _____ WHEN: _____

YOU: _____ WHERE: _____

US: _____

the last time we made each other laugh

HA HA HA!! ☺ HA!

ME: _____   WHEN: _____

YOU: _____   WHERE: _____

US: _____

our earliest memories
of each other

ARCHIVE

1.

2.

3.

something of yours
I wish I had too

ME: _____   WHEN: _____

You: _____   WHERE: _____

US: _____

something we changed our minds about

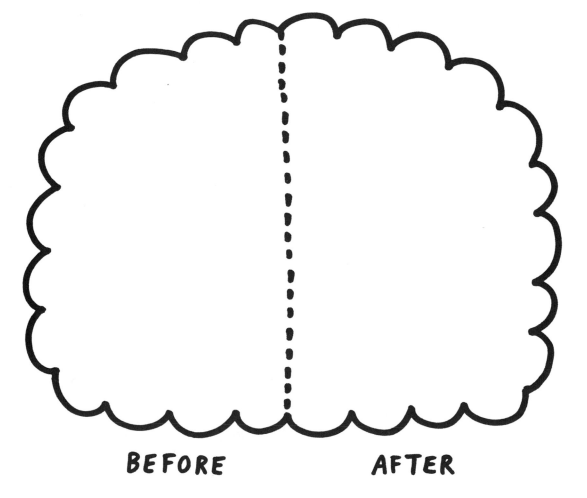

BEFORE   AFTER

ME: _____   WHEN: _____

You: _____   WHERE: _____

US: _____

the wildest adventure we've had together

DANGER ZONE!

ME: _____ WHEN: _____

YOU: _____ WHERE: _____

US: _____

messages from our inbox

ME: _____ WHEN: _____

YOU: _____ WHERE: _____

US: _____

where you can find us at a party

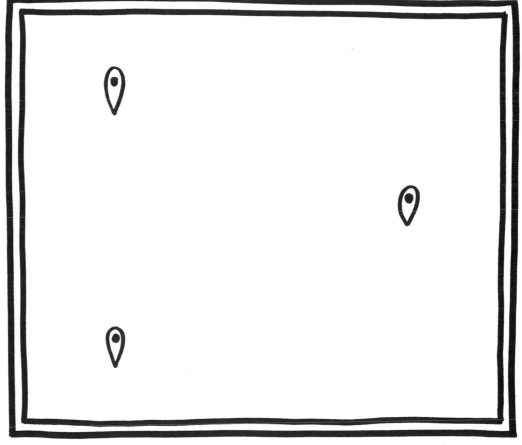

(& what we're probably doing)

ME: _____ WHEN: _____

You: _____ WHERE: _____

us: _____

a platter of our favorite comfort foods

ME: _____ WHEN: _____

You: _____ WHERE: _____

US: _____

that little thing we made a BIG deal about

CONGRATULATIONS!!

the fan mail we'd write to each other

OMG!!! hello!! ☺

always –
YOUR BIGGEST FAN!

ME: _____   WHEN: _____

You: _____   WHERE: _____

US: _____

♡ HELLO!!!   ♡ ♡ ♡   xx
                          ☺

L♡VE always xx YOUR xx
              BIGGEST x
                FAN ♡

ME: _____   WHEN: _____

You: _____   WHERE: _____

US: _____

last time we didn't act our age

☐ like little kids   ☐ like old people

ME: _____ WHEN: _____

You: _____ WHERE: _____

US: _____

someone I wish I could introduce you to

HELLO
MY NAME IS

HELLO
MY NAME IS

ME: _____ WHEN: _____
You: _____ WHERE: _____
US: _____

how we'd style our home
if we lived together

ME: _____ WHEN: _____

You: _____ WHERE: _____

US: _____

the questions we have for each other

HOW... ?

DO... ?

WHO... ?

ME: _____ WHEN: _____

You: _____ WHERE: _____

US: _____

our ^unofficial world record

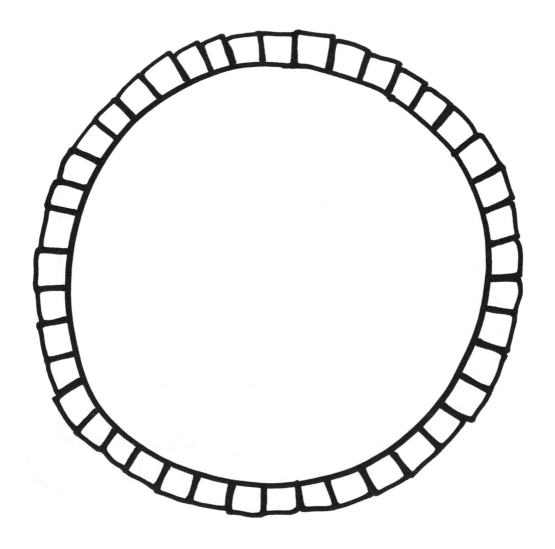

ME: _____ WHEN: _____

You: _____ WHERE: _____

US: _____

the life lesson we learned together

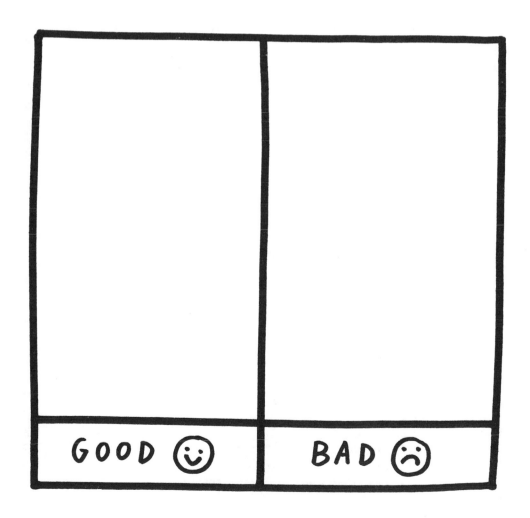

GOOD 🙂	BAD ☹️

ME: _____ WHEN: _____

YOU: _____ WHERE: _____

US: _____

the travel plans we
daydream about

BOARDING PASS

BOARDING PASS

ME: _____   WHEN: _____
You: _____   WHERE: _____
US: _____

an incredibly good
idea we had recently

ME: _____ WHEN: _____

You: _____ WHERE: _____

US: _____

things I couldn't have done without you

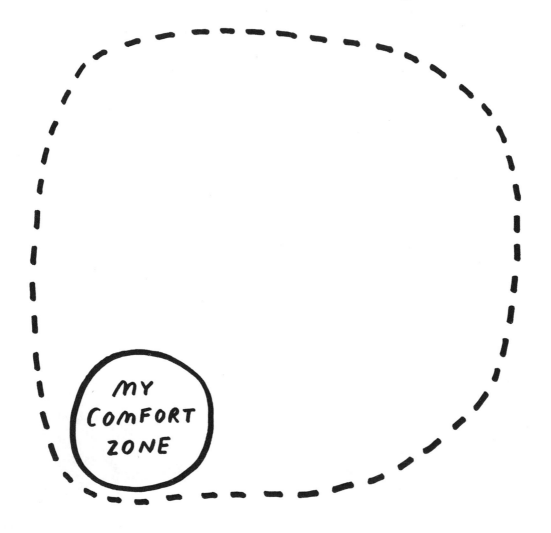

MY
COMFORT
ZONE

ME: _____   WHEN: _____

YOU: _____   WHERE: _____

US: _____

our new tradition

every... ☐ morning ☐ afternoon
☐ Tuesday ☐ full moon ☐ _____

ME: _____   WHEN: _____

YOU: _____   WHERE: _____

US: _____

how we exercise together

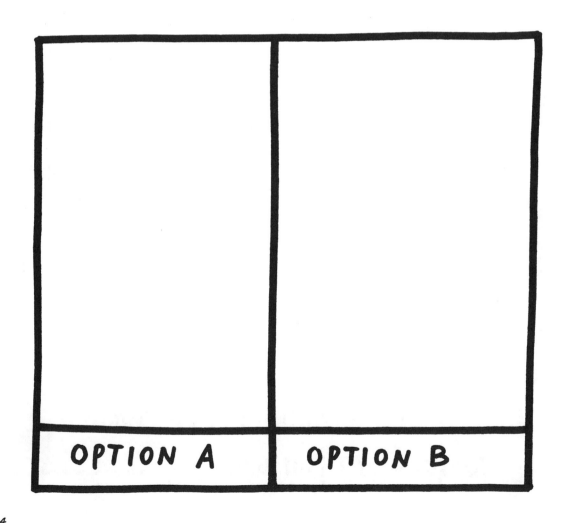

OPTION A	**OPTION B**

ME: _____ WHEN: _____

You: _____ WHERE: _____

US: _____

what we'd wish upon a star for tonight

ME: _____ WHEN: _____

You: _____ WHERE: _____

US: _____

we didn't want it to end!!

ME: _____ WHEN: _____

YOU: _____ WHERE: _____

US: _____

if we could live a day as any animal...

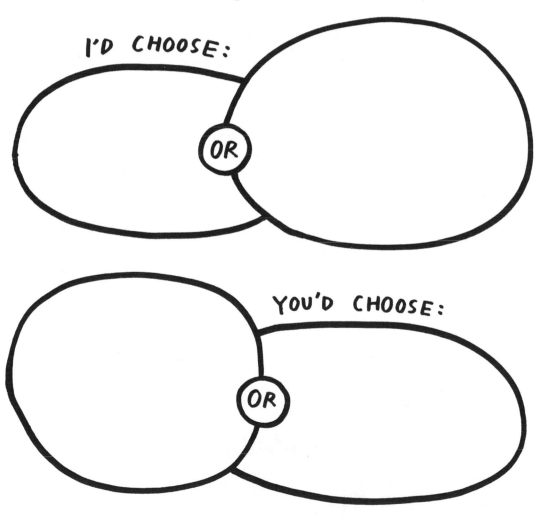

I'D CHOOSE:

OR

YOU'D CHOOSE:

OR

ME: _____ WHEN: _____

YOU: _____ WHERE: _____

US: _____

our good deed
for the day

☐ loud & heroic   ☐ small & sweet

ME: _____   WHEN: _____

You: _____   WHERE: _____

US: _____

a perfect
weekend together

SATURDAY

am:

pm:

SUNDAY

am:

pm:

ME: _____   WHEN: _____

YOU: _____   WHERE: _____

US: _____

if our names were
in the dictionary

_____

DEFINITION:

_____

DEFINITION:

ME: _____ WHEN: _____

You: _____ WHERE: _____

US: _____

things I'd be happy
to share with you

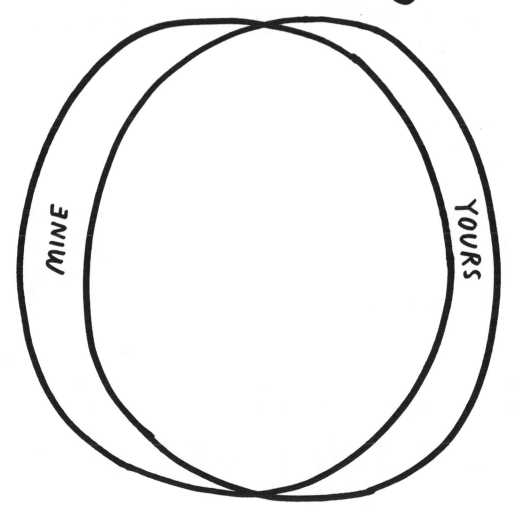

MINE

YOURS

ME: _____   WHEN: _____

YOU: _____   WHERE: _____

US: _____

an idea for the next sunny day we get

& a rainy day plan

ME: _____ WHEN: _____

YOU: _____ WHERE: _____

US: _____

we couldn't have done it without each other...

ME: _____ WHEN: _____

You: _____ WHERE: _____

us: _____

our recent transformation

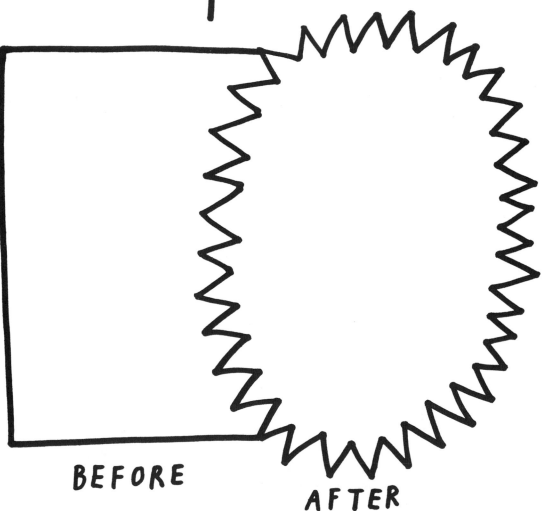

BEFORE

AFTER

ME: _____ WHEN: _____

You: _____ WHERE: _____

US: _____

memorable fashion choices from our past

ME: _____ WHEN: _____

You: _____ WHERE: _____

US: _____

an assumption we made about each other

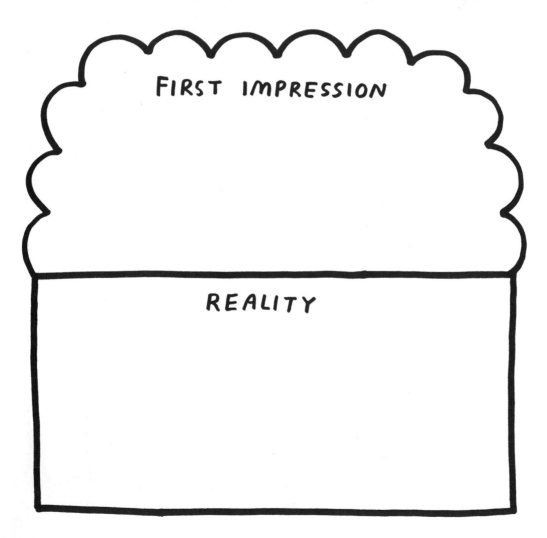

FIRST IMPRESSION

REALITY

what can instantly make our day better

ME: _____ WHEN: _____

YOU: _____ WHERE: _____

US: _____

the best advice we ever gave each other

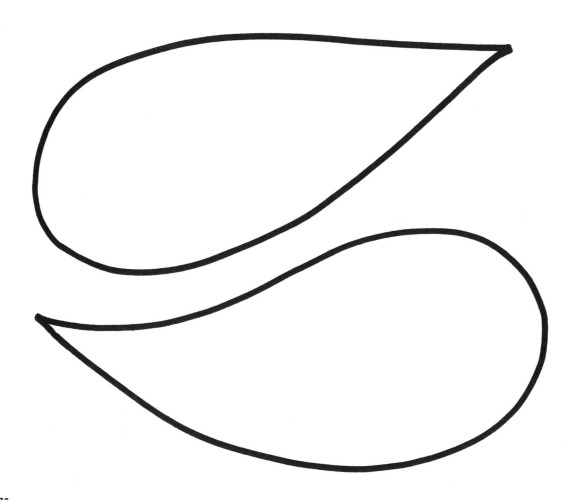

ME: _____ WHEN: _____

You: _____ WHERE: _____

US: _____

a favorite memory of us

ACCESS ONLY

BFF

LISA CURRIE IS A BIG BELIEVER IN THE CATHARTIC MAGIC OF PUTTING PEN TO PAPER, SO SHE MAKES BOOKS AND RESOURCES TO HELP PEOPLE DO MORE OF THAT. SHE SPENDS HER TIME BETWEEN MELBOURNE, AUSTRALIA, AND THE NOOK OF HER MIND WHERE DAYDREAMS ARE BORN.

LISACURRIE.COM

thank you!

☺ A big thank you to Marian and the team at Tarcher Perigee for making these books a real thing we can all doodle over.

☺ Thank you always to my agent, Sorche.

☺ Thanks Mum, for the encouragment and good vibes.

☺ Thanks to my housemate, Sarah, for co-creating a lovely space to make these books in.

☺ Thanks to my dear friends, Felicity and Chloe, who inspire me always and bring fun into my world.

☺ Thanks also to YOU, holding this book! It's my pleasure to make it for you. I often think about who you might be... and I hope that you (and whoever you share it with) have some fun here!

Also by Lisa Currie